ROWING

 BOY SCOUTS OF AMERICA.

Note to Counselors

Rowing merit badge instruction should follow the requirements, procedures, and techniques presented in this pamphlet. Learning objectives should emphasize safety and basic skill proficiency. The health aspects of aerobic exercise and the particular health and development benefits of rowing also should be considered.

The Rowing merit badge counselor should hold BSA Aquatics Instructor certification or should be trained in teaching skills and techniques by a currently certified BSA Aquatics Instructor.

The Rowing merit badge requirements can be completed either in fixed-seat or in sliding-seat craft. If a local council or camp has not yet acquired one or more sliding-seat rowing shells or drop-in units for canoe rowing, most dealers and manufacturers are willing to loan equipment for instructional activity. Some industry representatives also are quite willing to provide instruction. These opportunities and resources should not be overlooked.

BSA local councils are encouraged to add sliding-seat equipment to their summer camp rowing fleet. Sliding-seat rowing equipment has been immensely popular at BSA jamborees, and one reason for the revision of merit badge requirements was to increase Scout interest and participation in rowing. This revision also recognizes the rapidly growing popularity of competitive and exercise rowing.

35943
ISBN 978-0-8395-3404-4
©2006 Boy Scouts of America
2010 Printing

BANG/Brainerd, MN
3-2010/059117

Requirements

1. Show that you know first aid for and how to prevent injuries or illnesses that could occur while rowing, including cold and heat reactions, dehydration, contusions, lacerations, and blisters.

2. Do the following:
   a. Identify the conditions that must exist before performing CPR on a person. Explain how such conditions are recognized.

   b. Demonstrate proper technique for performing CPR using a training device approved by your counselor.

3. Before doing the following requirements, successfully complete the BSA swimmer test. Jump feetfirst into water over your head in depth. Level off and swim 75 yards in a strong manner using one or more of the following strokes: sidestroke, breaststroke, trudgen, or crawl; then swim 25 yards using an easy, resting backstroke. The 100 yards must be completed in one swim without stops and must include at least one sharp turn. After completing the swim, rest by floating.

4. Review and discuss Safety Afloat and demonstrate the proper fit and use of personal flotation devices (PFDs).

5. Do ONE of the following:
   a. Alone or with a passenger, do the following correctly in either a fixed-seat or sliding-seat rowboat:

   (1) Launch.

   (2) Row in a straight line for a quarter mile. Stop, make a pivot turn, and return to the starting point.

        (3) Backwater in a straight line for 50 yards. Make a turn under way and return to the starting point.

        (4) Land and moor or rack your craft.

        (5) Tie the following mooring knots—clove hitch, roundturn with two half-hitches, bowline, Wellman's knot, and mooring hitch.

  b. Participate as a rowing team member in a competitive rowing meet. The team may be sponsored by a school, club, or Scout unit. The meet must include competition between two or more teams with different sponsors. Complete at least 10 hours of team practice prior to the meet.

6. Do ONE of the following:

  a. In a fixed-seat rowboat, come alongside a dock and help a passenger into the boat. Pull away from the dock, change positions with your passenger, and scull in good form over the stern for 10 yards, including at least one 180-degree turn. Resume your rowing position, return alongside the pier, and help your passenger out of the boat.

  b. In a sliding-seat rowboat, come alongside a pier and, with your buddy assisting you, get out onto the pier. Help your buddy into the boat. Reverse roles with your buddy and repeat the procedure.

7. Participate in a swamped boat drill including righting and stabilizing the craft, reboarding in deep water, and making headway. Tell why you should stay with a swamped boat.

8. Alone in a rowboat, push off from the shore or a dock. Row 10 yards to a swimmer. While giving instructions to the swimmer, turn the boat so that the swimmer can hold on to the stern. Tow him to shore.

9. Show or explain the proper use of anchors for rowboats.

10. Describe the following:

   a. Types of crafts used in commercial, competitive, and recreational rowing.

   b. Four common boatbuilding materials. Give some positive and negative points of each.

   c. Types of oarlocks used in competitive and recreational rowing.

11. Discuss the following:

   a. The advantage of feathering oars while rowing

   b. Precautions regarding strong winds and heavy waves, and boat-handling procedures in rough water and windstorms

   c. How to properly fit out and maintain a boat in season, and how to prepare and store a boat for winter

   d. How to calculate the weight a boat can carry under normal conditions

   e. The differences between fixed-seat and sliding-seat rowing

   f. The different meanings of the term *sculling* in fixed- and sliding-seat rowing

   g. The health benefits from rowing for exercise

Contents

Rowing Through History

Oars, as a means of propelling boats, have been used for many centuries. People used rowing for river and coastal transportation and with sails for open-sea travel. As civilizations developed around the eastern end of the Mediterranean Sea, rowing became competitive. The cultures with the best rowers had an advantage in trade and military campaigns.

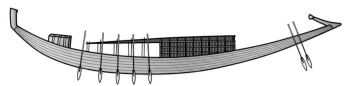

Archaeologists have found two funeral barges, such as the one shown here, buried in pits at the base of the Great Pyramid near Cairo, Egypt. They are from about 3500 B.C. These barges are one of the earliest examples of rowing.

Until the introduction of gunpowder and cannons, soldiers on war vessels had switched to oar power to maneuver close enough to an enemy ship for archers to shoot the sailors and to ram and sink the vessels.

A sketch of this style of war vessel, a *trireme*, has been found on Grecian pottery that scientists date to 900 B.C. The triremes had three banks of oars on each side and used about 200 rowers.

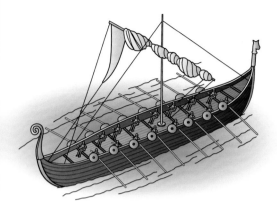

The Vikings used this type of boat to explore Iceland, Greenland, and the northern coast of North America.

As navigation techniques improved and vessels no longer had to follow the coastline to avoid getting lost, sailing ships increased in size and the use of oars decreased. People used rowboats to transport cargo and people between the shore and a larger ship. Rowboats also were used as fishing vessels. In addition, sailing ships carried rowboats of various sizes to use for transportation when they were docked in port, for battles that took place near shore, and for pulling the ship when the wind was calm.

Modern competitive rowing began around 1715 on the Thames River in London, England. By the early 1800s, amateur competition had become popular between Oxford and Cambridge universities in England. In the mid-1800s, amateur rowing competition spread to North America, where it gained popularity at East Coast colleges.

Sliding-seat rowing began as an effort by rowers to have a longer stroke and to use the strength of their legs. Originally, they wore greased leather pants so that they would be able to slide on a smooth plank. Eventually, someone invented a small seat with rollers that followed a set of tracks in the bottom of the boat.

The popularity of rowing competitions grew significantly in the 1980s and 1990s. Television broadcasts of Olympic rowing competitions have greatly increased public awareness of the sport. Recreational rowing also grew because of the public awareness of rowing competition and the health benefits it offers.

Rowing is the oldest college sport in the United States.

Sliding-seat rowing is one of the best forms of whole-body aerobic exercise. The popularity of rowing machines reflects the effectiveness of the skill as a fitness program, even on dry land.

There are more rowing opportunities than ever as schools, places of worship, and community clubs sponsor rowing teams in increasing numbers.

Commercial outfitters use large rafts that are controlled and guided by large oars. In the western United States, dory-style boats are used for river running and fishing.

First Aid

Rowing, like most other sports, has its own set of precautions. Here are some conditions that could occur while rowing and that you should be prepared to handle.

Hypothermia occurs when the body's core temperature falls below the normal range. Any combination of cool weather, wet skin or clothes, wind, exhaustion, or hunger can lead to hypothermia. Watch for these danger signs: loss of muscle strength and coordination, disorientation or incoherence, and pale or bluish skin tone. In severe stages, shivering stops and the victim falls unconscious. Anyone who starts to shiver or who shows discoloration around the lips or cheeks should immediately be taken off the water, thoroughly dried and dressed in dry clothing, and moved to a warm place.

Heat exhaustion and *heatstroke* occur when the body cannot keep itself cool enough. Symptoms include dizziness, faintness, nausea, weakness, headache, muscle cramps, paleness, and profuse sweating. To treat heat exhaustion, have the person lie down in a cool, shady spot with feet raised. Cool the person with a damp cloth or a fan. Have the victim sip water. Recovery should be rapid. If the condition worsens, get medical help. Heatstroke is the extreme stage where *dehydration* (body water loss) has caused sweating, the body's natural cooling mechanism, to stop and body temperature to rise to dangerous levels. The pulse is extremely rapid and the person will be disoriented or unconscious. The victim must be cooled immediately through immersion or with cold packs, and the fluid level of the body must be increased. Treat for shock and seek emergency medical help.

Sunburn is a familiar condition commonly associated with boating. To prevent sunburn, cover up, use a waterproof sunscreen with an SPF of at least 15, and limit your exposure time. If you begin to redden or feel discomfort, get out of the sun.

Contusion is the medical term for bruise. Most bruises are not serious and are easy to recognize and treat. Covering the site of a new bruise with a cold compress or towel for 0 minutes will help reduce discoloration, pain, and swelling. Seek medical help for any bruises that include possible bone injury or any contusions on the head or abdomen coupled with sharp or persistent pain.

Lacerations and *abrasions* (cuts and scrapes) may occur while rowing or, more likely, while climbing in and out of the boat or loading gear on a rough dock. As in other situations, the wound should be cleaned, disinfected, and covered. For severe bleeding injuries, control bleeding with pressure or at pressure points and get medical help.

In rowing, *blisters* are most likely to occur on the hands. Pay attention to any tender or sensitive areas (hot spots) that indicate the start of a blister. You may be able to adjust or relax your grip to avoid friction on the sensitive area. If not, listen to your body and quit for the day. If you are prone to blisters, prevent them by wearing rowing gloves. If you do get a blister, cover and protect the area from further irritation.

Cardiopulmonary resuscitation (CPR) is a procedure used on someone whose breathing and heartbeat have stopped. CPR is required *only* when someone has no pulse, indicating that the heart has stopped beating. Someone's heart may stop in the event of a heart attack or drowning. CPR includes both chest compressions and rescue breathing (mouth-to-mouth resuscitation). The procedure provides the blood circulation and breathing that could save the person's life. CPR should *not* be performed on someone who has a pulse. A drowning victim may stop breathing but could still have a pulse. In this case, *rescue breathing,* not CPR, is the correct procedure to follow.

CPR is the important first response in the event of a cardiac emergency, and such emergencies can occur as the result of any strenuous activity. CPR is used in drowning accidents when submersion has caused respiratory and cardiac arrest. Someone trained in CPR should be included in every rowing outing. Only people qualified by practice under supervision of a trained instructor should attempt CPR.

Swimming Skill and Safety

When earning any of the aquatic merit badges, it is important to follow safety rules and use self-discipline and judgment. You will need to be a confident swimmer, able to handle yourself in deep water should you capsize. In addition, you must understand and follow the nine points of Safety Afloat. These guidelines were developed to promote boating and boating safety and to set standards for safe unit activity afloat.

Don't Forget Your Buddy

Whenever you go swimming, make sure you have a buddy with you. If you go afloat, the same rule applies—go with a buddy boat.

BSA Swimmer Test

All rowers must have passed the BSA swimmer test. The BSA swimmer test demonstrates the minimum level of swimming ability required for safe deep-water swimming, a necessary part of safe open-water boating.

BSA Swimmer Test

To qualify as a "swimmer," you must pass the following swimmer test. Jump feetfirst into water over your head in depth. Level off and swim 75 yards in a strong manner using one or more of the following strokes: sidestroke, breaststroke, trudgen, or crawl. Then swim 25 yards using an easy resting backstroke. The 100 yards must be completed without any stops and must include at least one sharp turn. After completing the swim, rest by floating. This qualification test should be renewed annually.

Safety Afloat

The BSA Safety Afloat guidelines were developed to promote boating and boating safety and to set standards for safe unit activity afloat. They apply to all rowing activities.

Qualified Supervision. All activity afloat must be supervised by a mature and conscientious adult age 21 or older who understands and knowingly accepts responsibility for the well-being and safety of the children in his or her care. Further, that person must be experienced and qualified in the particular watercraft skills and equipment involved in the activity and be committed to compliance with BSA Safety Afloat standards. There should be one such supervisor for each 10 people, with a minimum of two adults for any one group. At least one supervisor must be age 21 or older, and the remaining supervisors must be age 18 or older. All supervisors must complete BSA Safety Afloat and Safe Swim Defense training and rescue training for the type of watercraft to be used in the activity, and at least one must be trained in CPR. It is strongly recommended that all units have at least one adult or older youth member currently trained as a BSA Lifeguard to assist in the planning and conducting of all activity afloat.

Physical Fitness. All persons must present a complete health history from a physician, parent, or legal guardian to show that they are physically fit. It is particularly important that the supervisors know about medical conditions such as diabetes, severe allergies, epilepsy, asthma, or heart conditions so that they can take the necessary precautions to make rowing safe.

Swimming Ability. A person who has not been classified as a "swimmer" may ride as a passenger in a rowboat or motorboat with an adult swimmer, or in a canoe, raft, or sailboat with an adult who is trained as a lifeguard or a lifesaver by a recognized agency. In all other circumstances, the person must be a swimmer to participate in an activity afloat. Swimmers must pass the BSA swimmer test.

Personal Flotation Equipment. All participants in rowing activities on open water must wear properly fitted U.S. Coast Guard–approved personal flotation devices (PFDs). Type II and III PFDs are recommended.

Every Scout oarsman should study and understand the points of the BSA Safety Afloat plan. The complete text can be found in the *Guide to Safe Scouting.*

Buddy System. Participants in all rowing activities must use the buddy system. Every participant must have a buddy, and every craft should have a buddy boat when on the water.

Skill Proficiency. All participants in rowing activities must be trained and experienced in watercraft handling skills, safety, and emergency procedures. For rowing activities, participants must complete either a minimum of three hours of training and supervised practice or meet the requirements of a basic handling test.

Planning. All rowing activities require proper planning.

- **Float Plan.** Include in a float plan a summary of the rowing activity, along with current maps and information about the waterway to be traveled. Also note exactly where the unit will put in and pull out and what course will be followed. Time estimates should be generous in case of unexpected weather conditions and to avoid traveling under time pressure. Review the plan with others who have traveled the course under similar seasonal conditions.

- **Local Rules.** Determine which state and local laws or regulations are applicable, and follow them. Get written permission to use or cross private property.

- **Notification.** Share the float plan with parents of participants and a member of the unit committee. Notify appropriate authorities, such as the Coast Guard, state police, or park personnel, when their jurisdiction is involved. When the unit returns from the activity, notify all those who were given a copy of the float plan.

- **Weather.** Check the weather forecast just before setting out, and keep an alert weather eye. Know and understand the seasonal weather pattern for the region. Bring all craft ashore when rough weather threatens.

- **Contingencies.** When planning, anticipate possible emergencies and other circumstances that could force a change of plans. Identify and consider all such circumstances and develop appropriate alternative plans in advance.

Equipment. All equipment must be suited to the craft, to water conditions, and to the individual; must be in good repair; and must satisfy all state and U.S. Coast Guard requirements. Whenever possible, carry spare equipment and appropriate repair materials. Keep appropriate rescue equipment ready and available for immediate use.

Discipline. All participants should know, understand, and respect the rules and procedures for safe unit activity afloat. The applicable rules should be presented and learned before the outing and should be reviewed at water's edge before the activity begins. Safety rules, plus common sense and good judgment, keep the fun from being interrupted by tragedy.

Personal Flotation Devices

Whenever you participate in any rowing activity on the open water, you must wear a U.S. Coast Guard–approved personal flotation device (PFD). Here are brief descriptions about the different types of PFDs. Recreational rowers usually wear Type III PFDs.

Type I, Offshore Life Jacket. Type I devices are designed to turn most unconscious victims faceup. The device gives a lot of flotation in the chest, shoulders, and upper back areas. The Type I is not designed for recreational rowing but for passengers on cruising vessels, such as ferries on large bodies of water.

Type II, Near-Shore Buoyant Vest. These PFDs are designed to turn an unconscious person in the water faceup in calm, inland waters. Shaped like a horse collar, the Type II PFD design places all the flotation in the front and around the neck. While it is not as bulky as the Type I, the Type II can be uncomfortable for longer rowing trips but is adequate for short periods of recreational boating and instruction. Type II PFDs are recommended for closer, inshore cruising and can be used on boats of all sizes.

Every skill and maneuver discussed in this pamphlet must be done while wearing a PFD.

Type I

Type II

Type III, Flotation Aid. These devices have the same buoyancy as Type II PFDs and are designed to keep a conscious person in a vertical or slightly backward position but may not prevent an unconscious person from floating facedown. The Type III device has less turning ability than the Type II. Its more even distribution of buoyancy makes it more comfortable for water activities such as flatwater rowing. The Type III is acceptable for boats of all sizes.

Type IV, Throwable Device. Type IV PFDs are ring buoys and seat cushions with straps. They are designed to be tossed to a nearby person in the water and should never be used in place of a wearable PFD.

Type III

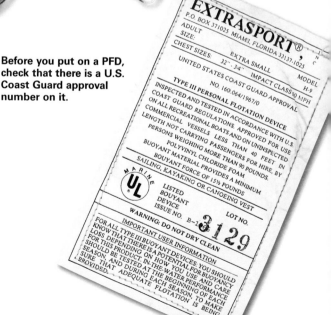

Type IV

Types II and III PFDs are acceptable for most Scouting aquatics activities.

Before you put on a PFD, check that there is a U.S. Coast Guard approval number on it.

18   ROWING

Sizing and Maintaining a PFD

To be effective, a PFD must be fitted and worn properly. Make sure that all side straps are adjusted to fit snugly, all ties are appropriately tied, all zippers are zipped, and all buckles are fastened. To check the fit, perform the shoulder strap test with a partner. Stand behind your partner and firmly pull up both shoulder straps. If you can pull the shoulder straps up to ear level, readjust the PFD or try a different style or size. In calm, shallow water, test the fit of your PFD by relaxing your body and tilting your head back. A properly fitted and sized PFD will keep your chin well above water. If it does not, readjust your PFD or try one with a higher buoyancy rating (found on the label).

Proper care and storage of PFDs is essential. Allow your PFD to drip dry, and store it in a well-ventilated place away from direct sunlight. Sunlight causes the fabric to fade and the flotation material to weaken. Never use a PFD as a kneeling pad or seat cushion, and never cut or alter your PFD. This includes gluing or sewing patches on the fabric that covers the flotation material. Finally, do not repair tears or holes in the material. If the fabric is ripped or if buckles are missing, replace the PFD.

Boats

For many years, almost all rowboats used in Scouting were fixed seat craft made of wood. Not surprisingly, a major part of BSA rowing activity involved repair and maintenance of these craft.

Most of the old, classic wooden boats that remain in the Scouting program are used only for display or maintained as collectibles. Some have been coated in fiberglass and kept in service. Most rowboats now available for Scouting activities are made of aluminum, fiberglass, plastic, or other synthetic materials.

Fixed-Seat Boats

Lightweight aluminum craft with built-in flotation (blocks of foam under the seats) are best suited and most economical for fixed-seat rowing. Unfortunately, there is limited demand today for fixed-seat rowing craft. Most new boats are designed for use with an outboard motor. As a result, these boats are often heavy and awkward for rowing.

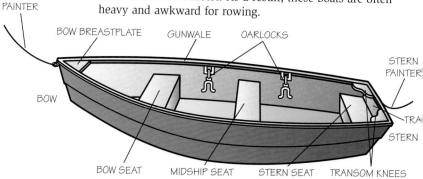

BOW PAINTER

BOW BREASTPLATE   GUNWALE   OARLOCKS

STERN PAINTER

BOW

STERN

TRA

BOW SEAT   MIDSHIP SEAT   STERN SEAT   TRANSOM KNEES

A lightweight aluminum dory skiff with two rowing positions, a stern seat, oarlocks, and a shallow keel or bottom runners is well-suited for fixed-seat rowing.

Punt—a narrow, shallow, flat-bottomed boat with identical square ends that have a sloping overhang.

Skiff—usually a small, flat-bottomed rowboat with straight sides, a pointed bow, and a transom stern.

Dingy—a small rowboat, usually round-bottomed with transom stern and used as a tender to a larger craft.

Pram—a short boat with a narrow, squared bow and a somewhat wider transom, typically 8 feet long with a 4-foot beam and usually V-bottomed.

Dory skiff—a shallow dory with the wide transom of a conventional rowboat.

Dory—a deep rowboat with a narrow, flat bottom and clinker-built sides that flare out to a relatively wide beam at the level of the gunwales. Dories have a sharp bow and a narrow, V-shaped transom.

Sliding-Seat Craft

Sliding-seat rowboats are characterized as either recreational or competition craft. Scouting activities commonly use the wider, generally heavier, and more stable one- or two-person recreational rowboats. Also recommended for merit badge instruction and practice are aluminum canoes fitted with drop-in, sliding-seat rowing rigs. Competition boats, usually called *shells*, are generally narrower, lighter in weight, sleeker in design, less stable, and more fragile.

Shell rowing consists of either sculling or sweep rowing. The term *sculling* can be confusing because it has different meanings in sliding- and fixed-seat rowing. In fixed-seat craft, sculling is done with one oar. In a rowing shell, sculling refers to rowing with two oars per rower. There are three sculling events in competitive rowing: single, double, and quad. In sweep rowing, each rower handles one oar.

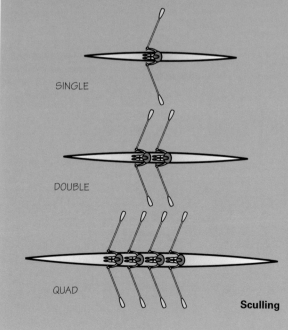

SINGLE

DOUBLE

QUAD

Sculling

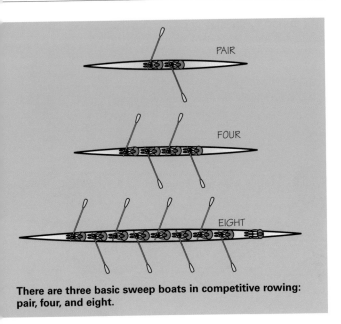

There are three basic sweep boats in competitive rowing: pair, four, and eight.

Recreational Craft

There are several types of recreational sliding-seat craft used in Scout rowing activities. They all have several basic parts: outriggers or *riggers* with oarlocks, a sliding seat on tracks, and a *stretcher* with adjustable footrests.

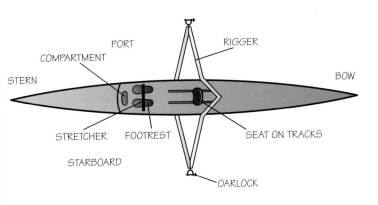

Two distinctive features of the rowing scull are the seat and the footrest. Sliding seats usually are contoured to reduce the risk of the seat slipping out from under the rower. The seat moves back and forth on runners mounted securely to the floor of the cockpit. The footrest secures the feet to a fixed position, which lets the rower use the legs to draw forward and to push back. The feet should be secured with hook-and-loop straps or lacing, which will permit the feet to slip free if the boat capsizes.

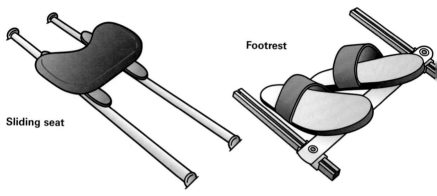

Footrest

Sliding seat

Canoe with drop-in rig

The Piantedosi unit can be attached in place in minutes by simply positioning the rig and finger-tightening the screw anchors to the gunwale.

Canoes with rowing rigs are especially well-suited for Scout programs because the craft can be used in canoeing and rowing programs. All you need to do to add a drop-in unit to a canoe is remove the midship thwart (the brace that spans the gunwales).

To adapt a canoe for tandem rowing, simply remove the bow seat and the midship thwart and drop in two rowing units. The unique features of the canoe as a rowing platform are its stability, compared with a shell, and speed, compared with a fixed-seat craft. A flat-bottom lake canoe works best, but the rowing unit can be fitted to almost any canoe configuration.

Boat Capacity

Avoid overloading or crowding a rowboat. Every boat has its safe limits of total weight and number of people. Many boats have a plate or sticker on the transom stating the capacity. Do not exceed the rated capacity for the boat.

You can use the following formula to compute the maximum number of people to be carried under fair-weather conditions in a fixed-seat rowboat.

> the length of the boat (in feet)
> ×
> the length of the beam (in feet)
> ÷
> 15
>
> The nearest whole number is the maximum number of people you should carry under normal conditions.
>
> A formula for determining the maximum safe load in pounds is:
>
> the length of the boat (in feet)
> ×
> the length of the beam (in feet)
> ×
> the depth of the boat (in feet)
> ×
> 7.5

Boat length is the keel measurement. The beam measurement is the width of the boat at its widest point, usually near midship from gunwale to gunwale. Depth is measured from the bottom of the transom to the lowest point on the top edge of the transom. If the transom is notched, measure from the bottom edge of the notch.

Safe load capacities apply to passengers and equipment. Usually, it is more reliable to use the capacity measurement in pounds. Do not attempt to carry passengers or equipment in a rowing shell unless it has a coxswain's seat or a storage compartment. A canoe rowing rig can carry the passenger and equipment load for which the canoe is rated.

Boatbuilding Materials

Rowboats are made from a variety of materials, including aluminum, fiberglass, plastic, wood planking, and plywood.

Aluminum. This lightweight, durable metal needs little maintenance. Aluminum will not float, but all approved aluminum boats have flotation materials in chambers that keep the boat afloat if it capsizes or swamps.

Wood Planking. Easy to cut and drill, wood is probably the easiest boatbuilding material to handle. It is very buoyant— a boat made from wood planking floats even when it is full of water. Cedar, spruce, cypress, and pine are good planking woods. Oak and ash are good for framing. However, to keep such craft watertight, they must be regularly caulked and painted.

Fiberglass. Extremely strong and durable, fiberglass can be used to coat a wooden boat. It will not rust, corrode, or dent, requires no painting, and is available in different colors. It is somewhat heavier than aluminum, and flotation material must be in chambers for safety. Some boats are molded completely from fiberglass.

Epoxy compounds also can be added to a wooden boat as a covering.

Plastic. Many recreational rowing shells and some smaller, fixed-seat craft are made of plastic. Plastic is generally lightweight, maintenance-free, and durable. Larger craft made of plastics, however, may lack strength and rigidity.

Plywood. Some people use kits or printed plans to build boats from marine plywood. Plywood is light, strong, and waterproof, and it comes in sizes large enough that the boats need only a few seams. Like boats built of wood planking, plywood boats must be regularly caulked and painted. They also have a tendency to splinter or split at the edges.

Boat Maintenance

Boats need daily maintenance. Maintenance tasks include washing the boat to remove dirt and grime; checking for leaks, loose rivets, nuts, and bolts; and looking for wear on the oarlocks. Respect and care for equipment will minimize maintenance problems.

All boats should be regularly washed and inspected for loose rivets, worn seams, and other signs of damage or wear.

A loose oarlock interferes with rowing and can quickly damage the boat. Check oarlocks and riggers before every use, and tighten as needed.

Rowboat Equipment

Standard rowboat equipment includes items such as oars, oarlocks, gate locks, outriggers, and anchors. Learning how to use the equipment on your boat is one of the first steps in becoming a skilled oarsman.

Oars

Except for the boat itself, oars are the most important equipment used in rowing. Learn to use and care for oars by first becoming familiar with their parts:

- The *handle*, where the oar is gripped
- The *loom*, or shaft
- The *throat*, where the loom meets the blade
- The *blade*, the flattened part that pushes against the water
- The *tip*, the end that dips into the water

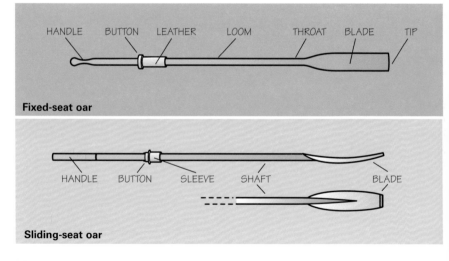

Fixed-seat oar
HANDLE   BUTTON   LEATHER   LOOM   THROAT   BLADE   TIP

Sliding-seat oar
HANDLE   BUTTON   SLEEVE   SHAFT   BLADE

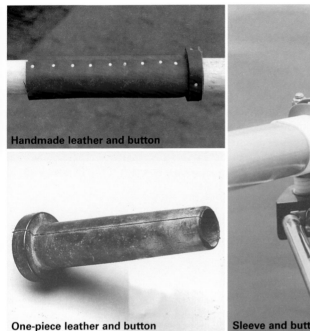

Handmade leather and button

One-piece leather and button

Sleeve and button in gate lock

Although a good oar is strong and durable, the part of the loom that comes in contact with the oarlock will wear out unless protected. You can add several years to the life of an oar by covering the area where the oar rests in the oarlock with a shield made of leather, rubber, plastic, or another synthetic. The shield should completely encircle an 8- to 12-inch segment of the oar. Often oars come with a shield or sleeve already in place.

The length of the sculling oar in sliding-seat rowing is usually 9½ to 10 feet. Sweep oars usually range from 12 feet to 12 feet, 8 inches long. Oars are manufactured in standard lengths in these ranges. Slight variances in length are used to accommodate the size and strength of the rower. For example, a high school crew will use a shorter oar than an Olympic crew.

The correct length of oar to use in a fixed-seat rowboat depends on the boat's beam (the width at the widest point) and freeboard (the distance between the surface of the water and the gunwales) and how the oar feels when you use it. The weight of your oars from handle to oarlock and from oarlock to blade should be almost balanced, with the blade end slightly heavier. The oar should be long enough to allow you to take a long, sweeping stroke when the blades are in the water. Recommended oar lengths for fixed-seat rowing are as follows.

Beam	Oar Length
36 inches	6 feet, 6 inches
42 inches	7 feet, 6 inches
48 inches	8 feet, 6 inches
54 inches	9 feet, 6 inches

Blade Types

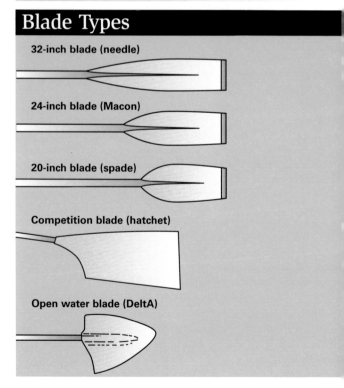

32-inch blade (needle)

24-inch blade (Macon)

20-inch blade (spade)

Competition blade (hatchet)

Open water blade (DeltA)

The area and shape of the oar blade are important. Until the late 1950s, blades were long and thin. They became known as *needles* and remain standard equipment in fixed-seat rowing. In the 1960s, however, a successful West German competitive rowing crew introduced a shorter, wider design called a *spade blade*. While the principle of rowing is to lever the boat past the blade, the blade is in fact never anchored at one spot in the water. This is because it slips as pressure is exerted. The idea behind spade blades is to reduce this slippage by making the blades shorter and wider. The wider the blade, the easier it is to get a firm hold on the water. However, the oar also is heavier and will result in greater drag.

The blades used most often today in competitive rowing are a combination of needle and spade. The most popular version is called a *Macon* because it was first used successfully in the 1959 European championships held in Macon, France. The Macon is slightly spoon-shaped, longer than the spade, and wider than the needle.

Competitive oars today also have curved blades to form a cup in the water. The greater the curvature, the less the slippage and the stronger the stroke. If the blade is curved too much, however, it is difficult to handle at the end of the stroke.

The Macon Blade

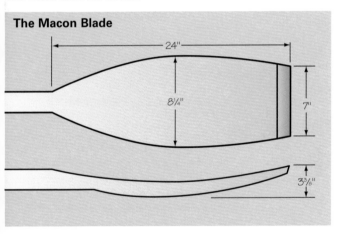

Oars used in fixed-seat rowing are usually made of wood. The sweep oars and sculling oars used in sliding-seat craft may be made of wood, aluminum, or synthetic materials such as plastic, fiberglass, or carbon graphite. Sliding-seat oars usually are hollow to reduce weight and are flattened on one side. The flat side is positioned against the side of the lock when the oar is being pulled. This shape also makes the oar more rigid.

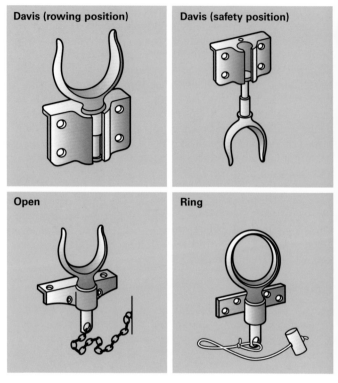

Davis (rowing position)

Davis (safety position)

Open

Ring

Oarlocks

The *oarlock* serves as a pivot point, or fulcrum, for the oar. It holds the oar in place. The earliest oarlocks were made of wood. By the early 1900s, dozens of types of metal oarlocks were in use. Today the choice of oarlocks is limited. The *Davis*, the *open*, and the *ring* are recommended for fixed-seat rowing because each of these swivels, allows feathering (placing the blade in a flat position, parallel to the water, before and during the recovery part of the rowing cycle), and can be lowered when not in use.

The Davis oarlock is self-contained. It is made out of bronze or galvanized iron. Flat, side, and angle sockets are available for the open and ring oarlocks. The locks should be secured with a lanyard or chain long enough for them to be lowered.

Outrigger and Gate Lock

Sliding-seat craft usually have gate locks on outriggers. The gate lock has a bar that closes the open part of the lock when the oar is in place. The gate bar is held in place by a lock nut. As the boat hull was narrowed for speed and weight reduction in competitive rowing, boat designers recognized that the fulcrum point needed to be maintained at some distance beyond the boat gunwale. Outriggers, or riggers, were developed for this purpose. The side of the lock on which the oar pushes during the stroke is squared off to match the flattened side of the oar loom.

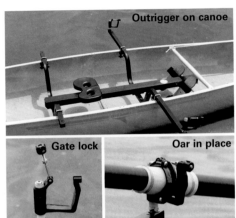

Outrigger on canoe

Gate lock

Oar in place

Sculling Lock

Some fixed-seat rowboats use a transom-mounted sculling lock or notch. You can buy a portable metal notch from boat suppliers, or you can make a portable notch by mounting a standard oarlock on a small wood block and mounting it on the transom with two C-clamps. Because the rower sits or stands in the center of the boat over the keel when sculling across the transom, the sculling notch should be set slightly off center to either side, depending on which hand the rower is using on the oar.

An advantage of the portable sculling lock is that it can be placed on either side of the transom or anywhere else along the gunwale. The sculling notch should have a small chain and hook that can be attached to the boat to prevent the lock from being lost overboard during mounting or unmounting.

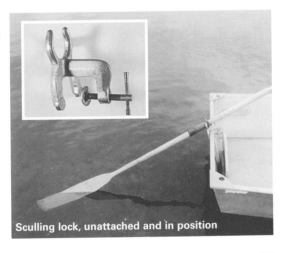

Sculling lock, unattached and in position

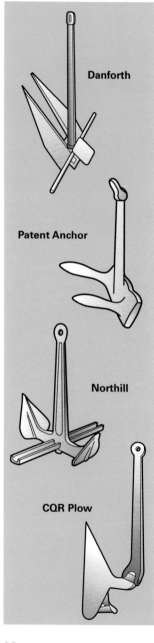

Danforth

Patent Anchor

Northill

CQR Plow

Anchors

If you plan to secure your fixed-seat boat on the open water for fishing or some other activity, you will need an anchor. The size of the anchor depends on the size of the boat, as well as the wind and water conditions. Bottom conditions usually determine the type of anchor you should use.

Many types of anchors are available. Different anchors have different holding power, depending on the type of bottom. Patent-type anchors are recommended, because they have great holding power for their weight. The Northill, Danforth, and CQR Plow are patent-type anchors. The flukes of these anchors bury themselves when tension is put on the anchor line. Sandy or muddy bottom conditions are best for patent-type anchors.

The grapnel anchor has four or five clawlike arms, curved upward, and is suitable when the bottom conditions are rocky or weedy. The mush-room anchor is a popular choice for permanent moorings. It has tremendous holding power when buried in a mud or sand bottom.

Either a drogue or a sea anchor can be used to slow the drift of a boat on the water. They can also be used to keep the bow of the boat into the wind. A drogue is a cone-shaped device that cre-ates drag in the water. A simple drag anchor can be made from a T-shirt.

For light anchoring, a homemade anchor can be made easily with a No. 10 can (a large coffee can), a large eyebolt, and some ready-mix concrete. Fill the can with concrete and set the anchor bolt into the center. One or more nuts on the anchor will help secure it.

The size and length of the anchor line depend on the size of the anchor and the depth of the water. As a rule, the length of the line should be seven times the depth of the water; however, this will depend on bottom conditions, wind, and current.

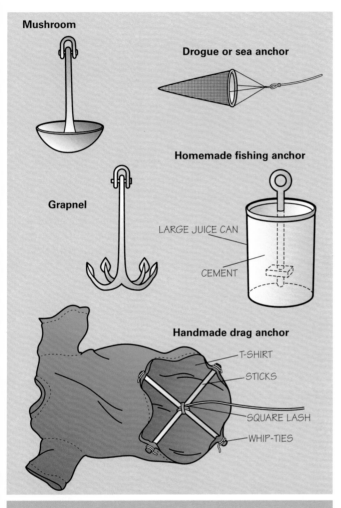

Mushroom

Drogue or sea anchor

Grapnel

Homemade fishing anchor

LARGE JUICE CAN

CEMENT

Handmade drag anchor

T-SHIRT

STICKS

SQUARE LASH

WHIP-TIES

Rocks do not make good anchors. They are easily dragged along the bottom by wave motion, wind, or current. It also is difficult to secure a rock to an anchor line.

Tips for Anchoring

- Always be sure the anchor line is secured to the boat before putting the anchor overboard.

- Always lower the anchor. Do not throw the anchor and line overboard together.

- Coil the line neatly when not in use.

Mooring Procedures

When your fixed-seat rowboat is not being used, it should be moored or secured to a dock, pier, or landing to prevent drift; damage by wind, wave, or tidal movement; damage to other craft; or interference with traffic on the water or at the mooring.

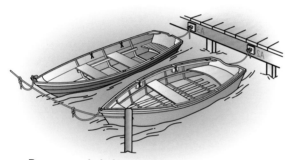

Recommended pier mooring

Moor rowing craft on the sheltered side of a pier with lines securing both the bow and the stern. Mooring lines should space the craft to avoid bumping and scraping. The best arrangement usually is securing the stern at the pier with the bow tied out so that the boat is suspended on the water, free of any contact. Always be sure that lines are secured so the boat will remain safely moored even if wind or current changes. Never leave an unattended boat secured with only one line. Three-eighths-inch stranded line should be eye spliced to the boat with the mooring end back spliced.

If the pier edge is properly cushioned to avoid damage, a rowboat can be secured safely alongside a pier with one gunwale against the protected edge of the pier. Bow and stern lines should be tight enough to prevent wind and waves from bouncing the boat against the pier.

Lower or remove oarlocks when the boat is moored. Secure all loose gear or remove it from the boat. Hang oars vertically to prevent bowing or warping the shaft. Avoid standing them on their tips or handles. It is easy to construct a permanent or improvised hanging rack, but if there is no place to hang your oars, it is best to lay them on a flat protected surface.

Unless safe and secure mooring on the water is impossible or impractical, do not haul heavy fixed-seat rowboats out of the water except for maintenance, cleaning, or seasonal storage. Outhauling stresses the craft and will shorten the useful life of the equipment. Dragging heavy craft onto the bank or dock will damage the boat's hull.

On the other hand, rowing shells, sculling craft, and canoes with drop-in units should be removed from the water when not in use. Store them upside down on racks where they are protected from sun, wind, and water. If shells are stored suspended on racks or in slings, be sure there is adequate support to prevent bowing or sagging.

In tidal water, mooring should permit the boat to rise and fall safely with the tide. Do not leave the boat hanging or grounded at low tide. During high tide, it should not be stressed by the mooring lines.

Mooring Knots

Several knots and hitches are useful in mooring your boat. The clove hitch, bowline, and roundturn with half-hitches are often used. For ease of release, the slippery clove, mooring hitch, and Wellman's knot are recommended.

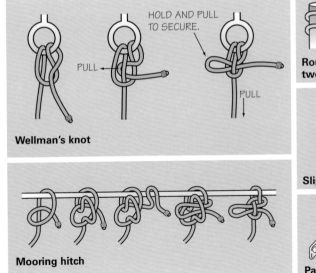

Wellman's knot

HOLD AND PULL TO SECURE.

PULL

PULL

Mooring hitch

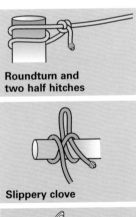

Roundturn and two half hitches

Slippery clove

Painter splice

Rowing Skills

Whether you are rowing in a fixed-seat craft or a sliding-seat craft or are rowing solo or tandem, there are a number of basic skills and maneuvers you will need to practice and master. Among these skills are boarding and launching, the rowing stroke, backing water, pivoting and turning, sculling, stopping, and landing.

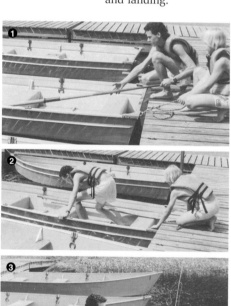

Fixed-Seat Tandem Rowing

Launching

If your fixed-seat rowboat is moored at a pier with the bow out, as recommended, a tandem launch is a simple matter of teamwork. Place oars and other gear in the boat over the transom from the dock before boarding.

After the gear is in place, untie the stern line (1). If you step into the boat over the transom while the stern line is tied, you stress the stern line and may damage the boat, pier, or line. The passenger should hold the end of the slack stern line while steadying the boat, either by kneeling on the pier and holding the transom with the hands or by sitting on the pier with the feet over the transom. If seated, the passenger should pull up on the transom with one or both hands while resting the feet on the transom seat. This will prevent the boat from rocking sharply if the person boarding gets off balance.

When the boat is steady, you, as oarsman, should step into the center of the boat from a sitting position on the pier and move forward to the bow seat, keeping low and over the keel (2). When you are settled at or forward of the bow seat, facing the bow, your passenger should push the boat out while continuing to hold the stern line, so that you can untie the bowline (3). After you have untied the bowline and brought it into the boat, you should move to the rowing position. If the water is unob-structed on both sides of the boat, you can set the oars out in the hold-water position to steady the boat. If oars cannot be used, then you should sit directly over the keel with a hand on each gunwale for maximum stability. When ready, tell the passenger to come aboard.

With the stern line, the passenger should pull the transom back to the pier and step into the boat from a sitting position on the pier (4). Immediately after boarding, the passenger should sit down in the center of the transom seat. If the passenger gets off balance or fails to keep centered while boarding, you should counterbalance by quickly shifting in the opposite direction.

When the passenger is settled and the stern line has been brought aboard, you are ready to row. If the mooring does not permit a rowing start, the passenger should push off gently against the dock (5). You should put out the oars when the boat is clear of the mooring.

If your boat is moored alongside the pier and there are no obstacles on the opposite side of the boat, you can board easily over the transom after repositioning the boat. First, untie the bow painter. Then, push the bow out and pull the transom back to the pier. With the boat in this position, the boarding procedure is the same as when moored bow out, except that there is no need to go forward to release the bowline.

If your boat is moored alongside the pier and the water is obstructed so that the boat cannot be swung bow out, you can board over the gunwale against the pier. Untie both bow and stern lines before beginning the boarding procedure. The passenger should kneel or sit on the pier with his feet over the gunwale near the transom (1). You should sit on the pier with your feet over the gunwale next to the rowing position. The passenger, while holding the stern painter to prevent drifting, should lean down and hold the gunwale to steady the boat. You should then step into the boat, and, keeping low, settle into the rowing position (2).

After you are settled and can steady the boat with one hand on the pier, the passenger should step in from a sitting position and settle into position on the transom seat. You can help by holding the passenger's hand or wrist for balance as he boards (3). The boat can then be moved along the pier by hand or paddled to open water where you can use the oars (4).

If your boat is sitting high and dry on the beach, you and your partner should stand on opposite sides, face each other, grasp the gunwales at midship, lift, and turn the boat so that the bow is toward the water. Walk sideways, being careful of your footing, until the bow can be set on the water. If the beach has a gradual slope, walk out into the water until both bow and stern are floating. If the water is not suitable for wading, stop at the water's edge, put the bow on the water, and pass the boat out hand-over-hand along the gunwales until the stern can be set on the water. While one person holds the boat, the other should load the gear. (If the gear is not heavy, it can be loaded before the boat is lifted from the beach.) If the water is shallow, walk the boat out before boarding to avoid grounding when you step in.

Another maneuver for getting under way from alongside a pier is to backwater, that is, row in reverse, with the outside oar, causing the boat to pivot on the corner of the transom against the pier. The bow will swing out as the transom rotates toward the pier. When the transom is flat against the pier, put out the other oar and begin rowing. This maneuver works only when the transom corner can press against the pier edge and serve as a pivot point and when there is room to swing the bow out in a wide arc.

As oarsman, you should enter first over the transom while the passenger steadies the boat. Keeping your weight low and centered, go to the rowing position and prepare to begin rowing. Then, steady the boat so the passenger can step in over the transom and settle into position on the transom seat.

Balance and Trim

For efficient and safe rowing, the boat should be trim and balanced on the water. If the boat is *balanced,* the port (left) and starboard (right) gunwales are the same distance above the water. This balance reduces the chance of tipping and spilling. For power and control, it also is important that the oars have the same angle and depth when rowing. If one oarlock is higher than the other because the boat is not in balance, rowing will be awkward and inefficient.

Trim refers to the way the boat rides on the water lengthwise. The bow should be slightly higher than the stern. If the oarsman rows from the forward position while carrying a passenger of approximately the same weight, the boat should be in trim. If the bow is low, increased drag will cause the boat to *yaw,* or deviate from its intended course, which results in more difficult, slower rowing. If the bow is high, the boat is not stable and wind resistance is more troublesome.

A correctly trimmed boat with single oarsman aboard

A correctly trimmed boat with an oarsman and a passenger aboard

A correctly trimmed boat with an oarsman and two passengers aboard

The Rowing Stroke

To prepare to row, place the oars in the oarlocks with the length inboard and outboard adjusted so that the handle ends almost touch each other as they pass at the nearest point. You will get more power in your stroke and will not tire as quickly, if the oar handles at the midpoint of the stroke are as near as possible to the centerline of both the boat and your body. This enables you to use your body weight and trunk muscles, rather than just your arms, in the power portion of the stroke.

Check your hand position by holding the oars in line just in front of you with the blades perpendicular to the water surface. The backs of your hands should be level. This level position should be maintained through the first part of your stroke. Hand position is essential for control of the blade angle and for feathering.

To determine the proper depth for your stroke, let the oar rest in the oarlock with the blade floating perpendicular in the water. The waterline on the blade in this at-rest position shows how much of the blade should be submerged when rowing.

For the catch and pull (figure A), the hands and wrists stay aligned in a level plane almost perpendicular to the blade angle of the oar. For the feather and recover (figure B), the wrists angle sharply down with hands up to turn and hold the oar blade parallel to the surface of the water. The line on the oar grip in the illustrations indicates the blade angle.

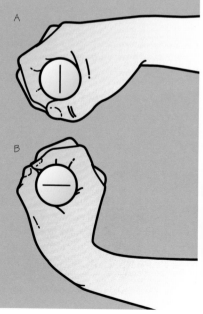

There are four parts to the complete rowing stroke: catch, pull, feather, and recover.

Catch

1. Catch—raising the handle of the oar so that the blade enters the water edgewise.

Catch. Sit with your back straight on the seat and grip both handles firmly, brace your feet about a shoulder width apart for power and balance, and keep your palms down. Bend at the waist and extend each handle an arm's length toward the stern. Your eyes should be straight ahead, and your wrists should be in a straight line with your arms. Raise the handles so that the blades enter the water almost vertically with the top edge angled slightly forward. This slight angle adds a little downward pressure to help keep the oar in the lock.

Pull. Begin by exerting a steady pull on the oars. Keep your arms extended during most of the stroke and bring the muscles of your back and legs into play with the weight of your body by pivoting from the hips. At the point where you are leaning back just beyond the vertical, complete the pull by bending your arms quickly, keeping your elbows in near your body. This final snap should pull your body erect.

By keeping your elbows near your body, you get more power for less effort and avoid lifting the oars from the locks at the end of the pull.

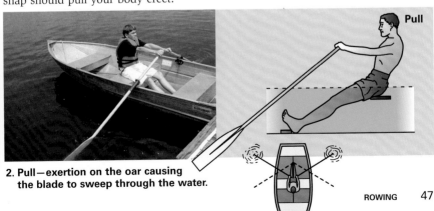

Pull

2. Pull—exertion on the oar causing the blade to sweep through the water.

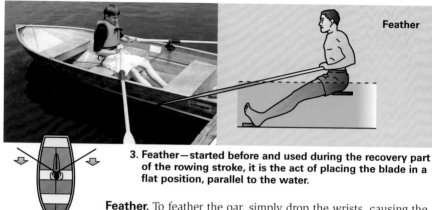

Feather

3. Feather—started before and used during the recovery part of the rowing stroke, it is the act of placing the blade in a flat position, parallel to the water.

Feather. To feather the oar, simply drop the wrists, causing the blade to turn parallel to the surface of the water as it leaves the water. Do not shift or let your grip slip on the oar handles. You should feather immediately at the end of the pull.

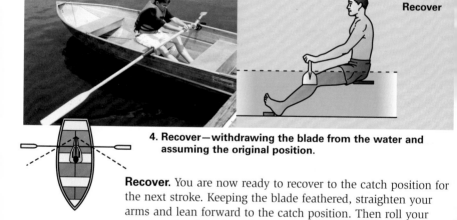

Recover

4. Recover—withdrawing the blade from the water and assuming the original position.

Recover. You are now ready to recover to the catch position for the next stroke. Keeping the blade feathered, straighten your arms and lean forward to the catch position. Then roll your wrists up level to place the oar blade in a near-vertical position. This completes the rowing stroke.

To avoid the more common rowing errors, remember the following:

- Avoid dipping the blade too deeply into the water.
- Keep your elbows close to your rib cage as you end the pull.
- Keep your hands at the same height.
- Keep your head level at all times.
- Pause briefly at the end of the recovery before the next catch.

A common beginner recovery error is to drop the hands below the knees, thus raising the blades high in the air. To start the next stroke you then have to lift your hands too high, forcing the oars too deep into the water. Rowing this way is clumsy and tiring, and it slows the speed of the boat. This "windmilling" also makes it difficult to keep the oar in the lock because raising your hands above the gunwales lifts the oar up rather than pulling it back against the side of the lock. Also, when the blade is dropped back to the water from a high position, the oar has a tendency to bounce out of the lock.

Rather than windmilling, move your hands back and forth as though in a groove. Keep them at almost the same height through the stroke. This way, the muscles do less work, the boat goes faster, the oars stay in the locks, and the rowing is smoother and more efficient.

During the recovery, be careful to keep the feathered blades tilted slightly up toward the bow and far enough above the water to avoid "catching a crab." This expression means allowing the forward (toward the bow) edge of your blade to tilt downward, while at the same time letting the recovery stroke dip too low, so that one or both oars dig into the water. The blade is thrust sharply downward, aided by the forward motion of the boat, driving the handle toward your chest in such a way that you might actually be knocked from your seat. If you do catch a crab while recovering, quickly roll your wrists up to raise the blade angle and the blade of the oar will plane back to the surface.

If you need to stop your craft from moving forward, dip both oars straight out from the locks and hold them firmly against the force of the water. This is called the *hold-water* position. Maintaining this position will reduce drift when the boat is stationary. For an even quicker stop, push forward on the oar handles from the hold-water position.

The easiest way to hold a straight course when rowing is to look over your shoulder and point the bow of your boat in the exact direction in which you wish to go. Then, looking over the center of the stern, pick out two fixed points on the water or shore that are in line as you look at them over the stern. As you row, keep these objects lined up and look over the bow occasionally to see that your way is clear.

If you need to alter or adjust your heading (direction), pull harder on the oar on the outside of the turn. For example, if you want to turn to the right, or starboard, pull harder with your right hand. If you need to turn sharply, pull hard on the oar on the outside of the turn and either let the oar on the inside of the turn drag or hold it straight out from the oarlock.

If you have a passenger riding in the stern, the passenger can serve as *coxswain*. The customary way for the coxswain to give signals is to make the following calls:

- *Prepare to give way* tells the rower to make ready to catch.

- *Give way* tells the rower to begin rowing.

- *Hold water* and *stop* both mean the rower should stop the boat.

Straight course with coxswain

An easy way for the coxswain to indicate direction is to put the palms together over the keel of the boat with the fingertips pointed in the direction the boat should be headed. When the coxswain's hands are pointed squarely at the rower, the boat is on course. The rower is thus able to watch the hand position of the coxswain and easily make course adjustments.

Backing Water

When you wish to make sternway (go backward) rather than headway (go forward), simply reverse the rowing stroke. Push instead of pull. This stroke is called *backing water.*

A rower may backwater when approaching the mooring. This procedure also is used for rescues and is a convenient way to approach the dock to pick up a passenger. You should backwater whenever you want to keep what you are approaching in sight.

Basically, the push stroke is the opposite of the pull stroke. You make the catch with your body arched back, your thumbs against your chest, and your elbows close to your body. To help maintain balance, brace one leg under or against the seat. To make the catch, raise your hands slightly, thrust your body toward the stern of the boat, bending at your hips, and extend your arms full length to complete the stroke. At the completion of the push, feather the oars by rolling the wrists up with the knuckles down, bringing the blades flat with the water and fairly close to the surface as your body swings back to begin another stroke.

To stop when backing water, dip the blades at the hold-water position and pull as needed. Turning when backing water is similar to rowing forward—push harder on the oar on the outside of the turn and drag the other oar as needed. Maintaining your course when backing water is easy. Simply point the center of the transom at your landmark and sustain that course.

Backing water—catch

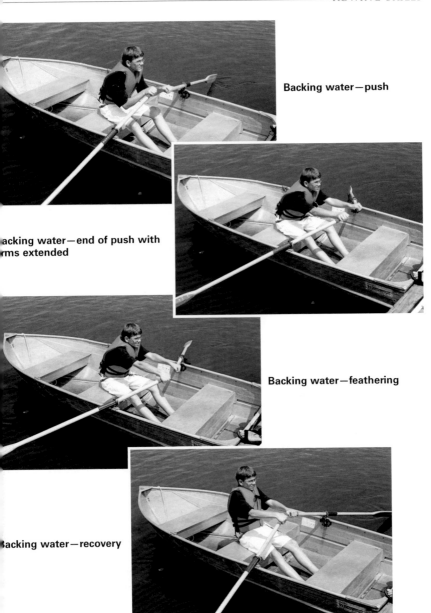

Backing water—push

Backing water—end of push with arms extended

Backing water—feathering

Backing water—recovery

Pivoting

Pivoting is an important skill in emergency situations when you need to make a quick reverse to approach stern first. A pivot also is used when coming alongside a pier or another boat.

To reverse direction as quickly as possible or to reverse while sitting stationary, you *pivot*. To pivot, backwater with one oar while doing a forward stroke with the other. When the maneuver is done correctly, the center pivotal point of the boat is practically motionless. Each oar catches at the same time, with the rower pushing and pulling in unison, finishing the strokes together. The oars are feathered and recovered at the same time to the original catch positions.

If you are pivoting to starboard, the starboard oar backs water while the port oar rows forward. If you want to do a port pivot, the port oar backs water while the starboard oar rows forward. Remember, for a starboard pivot, the right hand pulls (does a forward stroke); for a port pivot, the left hand pulls.

Pivot—catch

Pivot—push-pull

Pivot—feathering

Sculling

Sculling lets you move and maneuver a fixed-seat rowboat with single oar. Sculling also allows you to move and maneuver e boat while keeping one hand free for other things, such as hing. This skill also is useful if it is necessary to maneuver ur boat through a narrow or crowded waterway.

Sculling over side

Sculling over stern

You can scull from a seated position using the oarlock on either side of your boat, or over the transom from a seated or standing position. A transom sculling notch or a clamp-on sculling lock helps hold the oar in place when sculling over the transom.

Sculling from your usual rowing position will move the boat sideways. If you want to move your boat sideways to port scull with the oar on the starboard side. To move the boat to starboard, scull with the port oar.

For sculling over the transom, begin by practicing in a sitting or kneeling position. This keeps you low and more stable while you practice the sculling stroke. When you have a feel for the basic motion, practice in the standing position. Sculling while standing is less awkward because the oar has a sharper angle to the water and your arm can move in a plane at or just below shoulder level. The angle of the oar when sculling while standing gives more forward power. Another advantage is that from a standing position, you can look ahead and about in a crowded or narrow waterway.

To scull while standing, stand with your weight directly over the keel in the compartment or space between the transom and midship seats. Stand flat on the bottom of the boat with one foot on either side of the keel, but angle your body slightly to one side so that you can maneuver the oar over the transom while looking ahead. In general, you should stand diagonally across the centerline of the craft, facing the bow.

It helps to position your sculling notch off center on the transom toward the side your toes are pointing. Place the oar in the sculling lock and hold the handle with the hand nearest the stern. The oar should be held at about a 45-degree angle to the surface of the water with the blade submerged to the throat. Begin the sculling motion with the blade directly astern, the tip flat and parallel to the surface. Hold the oar with your wrist level and your elbow dropped naturally.

To begin sculling, drop your wrist and push your arm until it is extended full length in a line parallel with the transom. When your wrist is dropped, the blade turns from its flat position. As you extend your arm, the blade cuts through the water at an angle. The angle of the blade creates downward pressure on the blade, which you will feel as upward pressure on your hand. By holding your hand firm and level, this downward pressure on the transom pushes the boat forward.

sculling

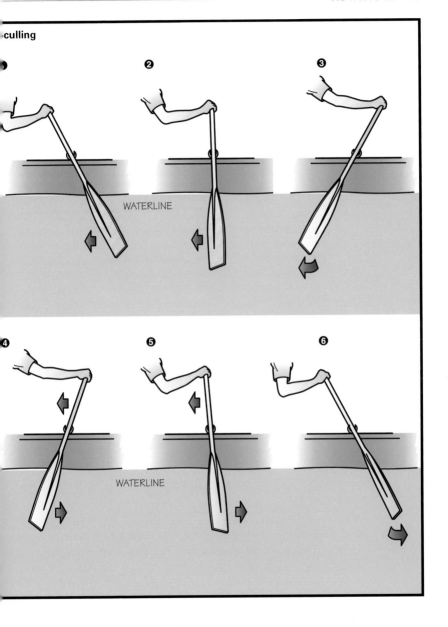

WATERLINE

WATERLINE

At the end of the thrust, raise your wrist to reverse the blade angle for the pull. The same side of the blade exerts pressure on the water on both the push and the pull portions of the stroke. After you have raised your wrist and angled the blade properly, pull back toward your shoulder as far as you can without feeling awkward or forcing yourself off balance. Keep your elbow low as you pull to move the oar handle in a straight line. The sculling stroke moves back and forth smoothly without pausing at either end of the stroke. Both your hand and the blade move back and forth in a straight line with no movement up or down. The only hand movement is at the end of the push or pull when the blade angle is shifted.

Practice sculling over the edge of the dock or on a practice board. If you have trouble with the blade motion, your instructor can stand in the water and guide the blade through the stroke by holding the blade tip while you hold the handle. You also could try using an oar with a mark on one side of the blade. Mark the side that exerts pressure on the water. As you practice, the mark should always be up and visible through the stroke. Remember that the leading edge of the blade as it moves through the water is always down.

Once you have learned the basic movement of the hand, practice without looking at the blade. Keep your eyes ahead and be confident that the blade is reacting correctly to the movement of your wrist. As in feathering, do not shift or let your grip slip on the handle while sculling.

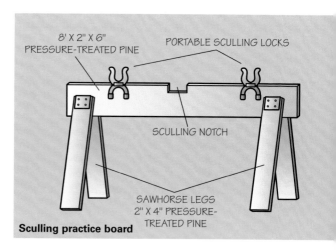

Sculling practice board

To turn while sculling, push or pull harder, depending on the direction of the turn. To make a sharp turn, pull or push hard and then recover for another stroke by feathering through the water. Feather through the water by keeping the blade angle parallel with the surface of the water and slicing back to begin another push or pull.

For example, if you are sculling in a standing position with your toes angled toward the port side of the boat and you want to make a sharp turn to port, pull hard on that portion of the sculling stroke. Feather through the water on the push, and then pull hard again. Repeat this process until you have completed your turn. If you want to turn to starboard from the same position, push hard and feather through the pull portion of the stroke.

To stop your boat when sculling, shift your hand on the oar so that you can hold it firmly against the transom, with the blade angle parallel to the line of the transom. Then raise the handle of the oar so that the blade pushes down and forward in the water just in back of the transom. If you are stopping suddenly, you might want to drop to a seated position and reverse scull.

When you have mastered the basic sculling technique, you will find that you can shorten the length of the sculling stroke to increase your forward speed and control. The shorter the stroke, the less the boat tends to zigzag when you are sculling.

Sculling has been used for years on the Chesapeake Bay by hunters in "sneak boats," moving from downwind to a flock of ducks. Hunters scull with a hand over their chests as they lie on their backs looking forward across the bow.

Reverse scull

Pull with bottom of blade against water.

Push with top of blade against water.

Feather.

Reverse Sculling

Reverse sculling moves the boat toward the side from which you are sculling. If you reverse scull over the transom, the boat moves backward. The principle is the same as in sculling, but in reverse sculling the underside of the blade exerts pressure on the water.

To reverse scull over the gunwale, sit on the center seat and place one hand at or just above the throat to hold the oar down against the water. Your upper hand should be at or below the handle, depending on what is comfortable for you. The movement through the water is the same as sculling, except you reverse your wrist action so that as the leading edge of the blade moves through the water it is angled up. This creates upward pressure on the blade and pulls the boat toward the blade. To extend your reach out from the boat, turn the blade perpendicular to the gunwale and slice or feather through the water, then resume reverse sculling.

Reverse sculling can be done from any position in the boat where the oar can be placed over the side. You will discover that you can scull simply by reversing the angle of the blade during the stroke. Reverse sculling takes more effort and is considerably slower than sculling forward in the standing position.

Because reverse sculling tends to force the oar up, you cannot reverse scull using only one hand in an open-top lock. Reverse sculling also is very difficult to do in a standing position.

hanging positions

Changing Positions

Communication and coordination are important when the oarsman and transom-seat passenger change positions. If you are
the oarsman, you should prepare for the procedure by holding
water. When the boat is stopped, bring in the oars and put
down the oarlocks. On signal, both of you should shift your
weight to opposite sides of the boat. This maintains the balance
of the boat while getting both of you in position to move.

When the boat is steady, on an agreed-upon signal you
both should move in the direction you are facing, keeping your
weight low, so that you pass side by side at about the midship
seat. The former passenger should move to the bow seat and
sit, keeping his weight on the side as before. When you reach
the transom seat, you should sit, also keeping your weight
shifted to the side. When both of you are seated and the boat
is steady, on signal you should shift to positions over the keel.

Pier Landings

If you are going to make a pier landing at a mooring where the boat is to be moored bow out, as recommended, row to a position near the pier and pivot. Backwater slowly into your mooring position until the stern is at or very near the pier. The passenger on the transom seat, holding the stern painter, should then make contact with the dock, get out, and either sit or kneel and hold the transom to steady the boat.

After bringing in the oars and lowering the locks, you should turn and, keeping low and balanced, move toward the bow and pick up the bow painter. The person on the dock should then gently push the boat out, holding the stern painter so that you can reach the tieline and secure the bow painter.

When the bow is secured, the person on the dock should pull the stern of the boat back to the dock and hold it steady while you hand out the oars and other gear. Keep all gear safely out of the way on the dock until the mooring is completed. When you are ready to step onto the dock, the person on the dock should steady the boat. Then secure the stern painter to the pier so that both stern and bow painters are taut and the boat is suspended between the bow tieline and the pier. Clear the dock of all gear and equipment and store it properly.

If you are going to make a pier landing by coming alongside the dock with the gunwale parallel to the edge of the pier, row at an angle toward the pier at the point where you want to land. Approach at approximately a 45-degree angle. The boat should have sufficient momentum to glide sideways to the pier after a partial pivot. When the bow is approximately one-half of a full boat length from the edge of the pier, you should pivot, swinging the bow into the wind or current and bringing in the oar on the pier side. If the pivot is executed precisely, the boat will have enough momentum to glide gently sideways up to the pier, where you can grab the pier. If the boat is about to stop short of the pier or is beginning to drift out of parallel, pull, push, or scull as needed with the oar still in the water.

If you are landing to let a passenger get out or for some other purpose while you remain in the boat, the oar away from the pier can be kept in the water to steady the craft and help hold the position at the pier. If you are mooring the boat, you should bring in the other oar. You and the passenger can get out of the boat by reversing the procedure used to board from alongside the pier.

Shore Landings

You can land a rowboat on shore, either bow first or stern first. If the water's edge is rough and rocky or if there is a sharp drop at the edge of the water, in most cases it is better to go in stern first. If landing bow first, row slowly toward the shore until the boat just touches the shore or the bottom in shallow water. Remember that wind or waves can drive the boat forward. You might need to hold back to prevent damage to the boat. A sudden lurch also could throw you or your passenger off balance and cause injury.

When the boat has touched shore, bring in the oars, drop the oarlocks, and step over the edge at midship into shallow water. Be sure of the water's depth before you step over. Keep your weight low and step over one foot at a time, carefully holding onto the gunwales. The passenger should help steady the boat by shifting his or her weight to counterbalance your weight. After you step out, the boat will ride a bit higher in the water. You can walk the boat slightly more toward shore and then steady it while the passenger steps out from approximately midship. If you are going to leave the boat, lift it from the water or tie it securely. Be sure you do not leave the boat where it can be damaged by wind or wave action or where it might drift free.

If you are going to make a stern-first landing on the shore, row to the shore until you are about a boat length out. Then pivot and backwater slowly until you make shore contact. Hold the boat steady with the oars while the stern-seat passenger gets out over the transom. Then bring in the oars, put down the oarlocks, and move carefully to the stern of the boat while it is steadied by the person on shore. After you step out over the transom, secure the boat.

ssisting Passengers

'hen you take passengers on board, you must tell them specif-
ally what you want them to do. As the oarsman, you should
e aboard first, seated on the forward seat and holding the boat
gainst the landing or pier. Ask the passenger to step aboard
idship as near the center of the boat as possible and tell the
erson where to sit to maintain trim and balance. If the pier is
igher than the gunwale of the boat, have the passenger sit on
e pier with his feet over the gunwale and then step down into
e boat from this position. If a boarding passenger needs more
elp to stay balanced, have the person step in just ahead of
our seated position while you hold the arm or hand closest
o you. Maintain dock contact with your other hand.

To unload a passenger, bring the boat alongside the pier.
emain seated while holding onto the pier, and ask the passen-
er to step ashore from midship. You can offer a hand to help
e person stay steady.

An alternative boarding procedure is to hold the stern of
e boat against the pier by backing water while the passenger
oards over the transom from a seated position on the dock.
s oarsman, you should be in the forward rowing position.
everse the process to let a passenger get out. While you hold
e stern against the dock by backing water, the passenger
hould get up from the transom seat and sit on the dock.

The over-transom
method does not
let you steady the
boat against the
dock or lend a
helping hand, so
use it only when
the water is calm
and you have
an experienced
passenger.

Fixed-Seat Single Rowing

The strokes and maneuvers of rowing alone are the same as rowing with a passenger, except that you sit on the midship seat to maintain trim.

Launching and Landing

When doing a single-person launch from a mooring where the bow is tied out, it is a good idea to ask another boater for help. The person assisting will play the role of the passenger except that instead of getting in when you are ready, he or she will give you a gentle push off.

If no one is available to help out, begin by loading your gear into the boat, then untying the stern painter. Sit on the dock and ease in over the transom while being careful to not lose your balance. Move forward to the bow and untie the bow painter. When the boat is free and you have pulled the painters into the boat, take your rowing position and move the boat away from the pier. If there is not enough space for you to row out, use one oar over the stern or at the bow to scull or paddle yourself clear of obstacles, then begin rowing.

If your boat is moored with one side against a dock or pier the procedures for getting under way are generally the same as when you have a passenger, except that you might not have any help. Push off or backwater to turn the bow out if there is enough open water. Otherwise, move along the pier by hand or hand paddle to open water where you can use your oars.

The single-person landing procedure is simply the reverse of the launch. Remember to tie the bow first and then scull or paddle the stern to the dock. Leave enough slack when you tie the bow rope so you can get to the dock.

A single-person landing or launch from shore is the same with or without a passenger, except that after rowing to the shore and bringing in your oars, you will have to move fore or aft or step over the edge with no one to help steady the boat. You will not have anyone to give you a push off after you are in position either. This means the boat might drift slightly after you have boarded and while you are preparing to row. A good way to avoid such problems is to scull or paddle the boat away from any obstacles before you take your rowing position.

When you are alone in a boat, any movement fore or aft or stepping in or stepping out, will push your boat in the opposite direction of your movement. For example, if you backwater up to a pier until your stern is touching, then bring in your oars and move from the midship seat to the transom seat, the boat will move out from the pier. If you anticipate this, you can bring in your oars while you still have some momentum toward the dock. Your movement in the boat will then counteract and slow your movement into the dock enough that you can make easy hand contact.

Single and Tandem Sliding-Seat Rowing

Merit badge requirements and sliding-seat rowing activities in Scouting reflect the practicality of single and tandem recreational rowing as well as the popularity of competitive crew rowing. You can meet some of the merit badge requirements as part of a competitive rowing team, but you will need to use a single or tandem craft to complete most. The following discussion focuses on single and tandem sliding-seat rowboats.

Launching

It is best to launch and board a rowing shell from shallow water. You will need a partner. Together lift at the bow and stern and walk carefully into the shallow water. Place the boat parallel to the shore in water with a depth between your knees and thighs. Point the bow away from shore. You can position seats, footrests, and outriggers while the boat is sitting near the water's edge, or they can be positioned after the boat is on the water. Set oars in the locks after the boat is on the water. When all equipment is in place, you are ready to board.

Stand close to the side of the boat, in line with the seat and facing the shore. Position the oars so they are straight out from the boat on each side with the blades lying on the water in the feathered position. The oars will stabilize the boat. When you hold the handles together over the center of the boat, the oars act as outriggers, and it is virtually impossible to capsize the boat.

With the hand closest to the boat, grasp the handles of both oars so that they are locked together. Raise the leg nearest the boat and place your foot squarely in the center of the boat just ahead of the seat runners (1). Then put your weight on the foot that is in the boat so that you can lift yourself up over the side. Sit down quickly on the seat (2). If you keep a firm grip on the oar handles, the boat will not tip. The last leg to come into the boat should be extended immediately against the foot brace. Don't worry at this point about trying to slip your foot into the straps. Extend the other leg and place it against the foot brace.

Take a moment to get settled and feel how the boat balances. You can rock the boat side to side by gently seesawing the oar handles. Scoot your seat all the way forward into a tuck position with the oar handles between your chest and knees. Then reach over the oars with both arms and hold the oar handles under your arms with the handle tips together against your chest and just beneath your chin. This allows you to keep the oars in position to prevent tipping while you reach across to secure your foot straps (3).

When your feet are securely in place (3a), extend your
~s and grip the oar handles with your hands. The oar han-
~s should overlap so that the left hand is over the right (4).
~tate the oars so that the blades are at right angles to the
~ter (with the tips curving toward the stern) and check your
~nd position. Your hands are properly placed with the oars in
~s position if the backs of your hands are flat with the knuck-
~ forward. Curve your thumbs over the end of the handles
~). This keeps the thumb on the upper hand from dragging
~ross or getting pinched against the lower hand. This also
~sumes that your hands are at the ends of the handles, where
~u have the greatest leverage.

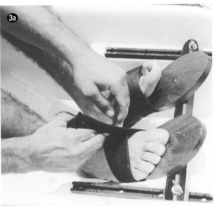

**Adjustable straps enable you to pull back
to your "catch" position, and you can easily
slip your feet out if the boat capsizes.**

When you are first practicing the procedure for getting in and out of the
boat, it is a good idea to have someone help you stabilize the boat by
holding the rigger. Your instructor can help you until you are confident
of both your balance and the procedure.

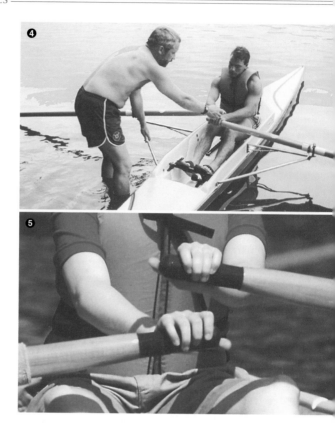

Balance

When your hands are directly in front of you, left over right, and the oars are straight out with the blades on the water, you are in the *safety position*. If you hold this position, the boat will not tip. Anytime you feel awkward, uncomfortable, or unbalanced or when you just want to stop and think or rest, move into the safety position.

When you are in the safety position, the boat is very stable. If you let go of the oars, however, the craft will be very unstable. If you need one hand free to reach for something or to make an adjustment, be sure to grasp the oars firmly together with the other hand. If you need both hands free, pull forward and lock the oars together against your chest, as you did when you were adjusting your foot straps.

The Rowing Stroke

The rowing stroke for a sliding-seat boat has the same elements as for a fixed-seat rowboat. The pull, however, is more of a push with the legs, with your back and arms coming into play later in the stroke. This leg push takes less effort and adds more power, as compared with the fixed-seat rowboat stroke.

For the catch position, pull yourself all the way forward, with your arms straight out ahead of you and your knees pulled up to your chest, knees almost touching. Your upper body should be leaning slightly forward over your knees.

When you have made your catch and are ready to apply power, push with your legs, keeping your arms straight until your legs are extended. Do not lift up. Keep your hands level, pulling in a straight line as your legs extend. When your legs are fully extended, your body should be leaning slightly backward toward the bow, with your arms straight. At this point, pull straight back with your arms for about five or six inches, keeping your elbows close to your ribs, to the end of the stroke.

Sliding-seat rowing—catch

Sliding-seat rowing—push with legs

Sliding-seat rowing—finish push

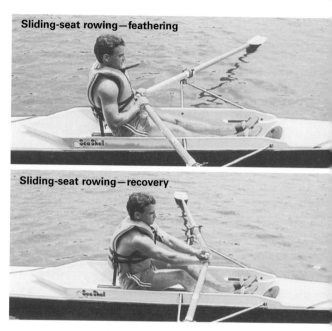

Sliding-seat rowing—feathering

Sliding-seat rowing—recovery

Feather by dropping your wrists so that the blades are flat on the water, with the edge toward the bow slightly higher. Recover with the oars slipping across the top of the water. Do not raise the oars out of the water or the boat will tip. Just as you kept your hands level and moving in a straight line as you exerted power, keep your hands in the same line and moving straight out in front of you when feathering.

When you are first learning the rowing stroke, make your stroke very slow and concentrate on moving your hands in a horizontal line. Keep your stroke relatively short. When you become more confident and experienced in the boat, you can lengthen your stroke by reaching farther out for the catch, using more of a pull with your back after your legs are extended, and bringing your hands farther back at the end of the stroke.

During the recovery, you can carry the oars slightly off the water to let the shell glide without the friction of the oars on the water. As you arrive at the catch, rotate the oar to prepare it for entry into the water, then lift your hands very slightly to place the blade in the water.

topping

ou can stop a shell very quickly by bringing the oars to the
fety position and dipping them with the blades almost per-
ndicular to the surface of the water. (If the blades are pre-
sely perpendicular to the water and the boat has any speed,
e oars could be ripped out of the rower's hands.) Hold them
mly in position in the water. To stop even more quickly,
p in this position and push slightly forward on the handles.

rns and Pivots

o turn under way in a rowing shell, hold the oar on the
side of the turn straight out, in the feather position, and on
e surface of the water while making short forward strokes
ith the other oar. The pivot maneuver in a rowing shell is
milar to making a turn, except that you stroke with both
rs. Begin in the safety position with both legs extended.
o not use your legs when making the pivot. Pull on one oar
hile backing water with the other, as in a fixed-seat rowboat,
ut make only short strokes. The handles of the oars should
ove a maximum of 12 to 15 inches (or arm's length) and
en feather back to make another short stroke.

If you pull hard
on one oar while
pushing on the
other, you will
likely capsize,
because you
will have no
oar extension
to maintain your
stability and
equilibrium.

Pivot—catch

Pivot—push and pull

Shore Landing

To land a shell, approach the shore until you are on water that is about thigh deep, and pivot the boat until you are parallel to the shore. Stop, and then reverse the procedure you followed when you got into the boat. Maintaining the safety position with your oars, release your foot straps and step out one leg at a time while holding the oars together in the safety position with one hand.

With most shells you can cross the oar blades on the deck just ahead of the cockpit, lift the boat out of the water, and set it safely up on the beach with all rigging in place. You will need two people to do this. Together lift at the bow and stern and walk out carefully. This makes it quicker and easier to put the boat back on the water when you are ready to resume rowing. If you are through for the day or are going to be off the water for some time, remove the oars from the locks and place both oars and the shell on a rack or in another safe area.

Never leave a shell unattended on the water.

Dock Landing

You also can land your shell at a dock. Docks at rowing clubs may be specially built low to the water so you can bring your shell in broadside with the deck below the rigger. If so, you can approach and land much as you would to do a dock landing in a fixed-seat rowboat. However, instead of bringing in the dock-side oar, you should lift the blade so that oar and rigger go in over the dock. When the shell is alongside the dock and is held steady by a buddy, lift your weight off the seat and turn 90 degrees to a sitting position on the dock.

Position the shell at the dock corner.

With the outside hand holding both grips, place the other hand on the dock and move the feet under the body.

Press down on the dock and oar grips while lifting weight off the seat.

Rotate the body to sit on the dock corner.

In most cases, however, the dock will be higher than your rigger, and you will need to make your approach and landing at a corner, with only the front half of your shell alongside the dock. Hold water and gently coast up to where the dock corner fits into the right angle formed where the rigger meets or crosses the side of the shell (1).

When you are in position at the dock, hold the oars in the locked position with the hand away from the dock, and place the hand nearest the dock on top of the dock corner (2). While a buddy steadies the bow, lift your weight off the seat by pressing down on the oar grips and the dock (3). From this position, turn and sit on the edge of the dock (4). To board from a dock, reverse the procedure while a buddy holds and steadies the shell.

Be sure there are no people or objects on the dock that the oar might hit.

Backing Water

To backwater, or reverse, sit up straight with the oars in the safety position, catch at that position, and push forward using only your arms. Make short strokes and feather back for another catch.

Sliding-seat rowing — backing water

Rescue Procedures

Being prepared to handle emergencies while out rowing makes activities on the open water safer and more fun for everyone. Considerate boatsmanship includes rendering assistance promptly to other rowers or swimmers in distress.

Overboard Procedures

If your fixed-seat rowboat swamps or capsizes, stay with the boat. Do not attempt to swim to shore. A boat's buoyancy—even when full of water—can support you and several others. Your PFD will keep you afloat safely. If the air and water temperatures are warm and there is no risk of losing your grip, you are safe hanging on to the side of the boat. However, it is usually a good idea to get back in the boat. Then there is no chance that you will lose your grip and be swept away by wind or current.

Although the water temperature may not feel uncomfortable, long immersion while holding on to the side of the boat could bring on hypothermia.

Approaching the shore

If you are with a friend and your boat capsizes, pull yourself up over the side of the swamped boat while your friend holds down the other side. Push down on the gunwale with both hands so that you bring yourself up to where your hips are about level with the gunwale. Don't rush. Then roll over so that you fall into the bottom of the swamped boat, landing on your backside. You can then lean over the side to counterbalance as your friend follows the same steps to come in over the opposite side.

Remember that when you pull yourself up on the gunwale, the gunwale will be forced down into the water. After you roll in and get your weight off the gunwale, it will rise back up. Even when fully awash, the gunwale of most boats will be a few inches above the level of the water.

Once in the boat, sit as low as possible directly over the keel. One person should sit on the boat bottom just ahead of the transom seat with the legs against or over the midship seat. The other should sit with his head at the bow and his feet against or over the bow seat. Facing each other makes it easier to communicate and to see where you are.

The safest and least tiring way to move a swamped rowboat to shore is to use your oar like a paddle or to hand paddle while sitting low in the boat. Remember that balance is important in a swamped boat. Any off-center movement will cause the water in the boat to shift, and may roll the boat on its side, dumping you out. Keep your weight low and over the keel.

If you have swamped and your boat is floating bottom up, get on one side and lift up on the gunwale. After you break the air seal, the boat may roll over on its own. If not, swim forward, pushing the gunwale ahead of you, and the boat might roll over, coming up under you so that you are in the boat when it is right side up. You and a buddy can work together on this maneuver. Another way is to push down on the gunwale while pulling the keel toward you. As the boat begins to roll toward you, hand walk across the bottom to the gunwale on the far side and bring it over. If a line or long painter is handy, secure one end to an oarlock and throw the line over the boat bottom. From the opposite side, pull the line to you and walk the bottom of the boat over to an upright position.

If you are alone and your boat swamps and you go over the side, the best way to get back in is over the transom. If you keep your body weight directly over the center of the transom, you can pull yourself up and roll in.

If there is a long distance to be traveled, take turns in and out of the boat to avoid fatigue. Anyone who is cold, weak, or injured should be kept in the boat. In cool or cold water, keep clothing on to prevent hypothermia. If weather conditions permit, you may remove certain clothing (such as shoes) to make swimming easier.

Never let go of the boat and swim off to pick up equipment. You can always get the equipment after you are back in the boat. The wind can move a boat that is floating free very rapidly across the water. If you lose contact, you might not be able to catch up with the boat.

If you are rowing alone and are thrown out or fall overboard while the boat remains afloat, grab the boat as quickly as possible and hang on. To get back in, move to the stern. Keep your weight at the center of the transom while pulling yourself up with your arms and performing a strong kick in the water until the top edge of the transom is about at your waist. Drop your head and roll over so that you fall back first or bottom first onto the transom seat. Your legs from the knees down will be hanging over the transom or the gunwale next to the transom. Rest momentarily in this position until the boat steadies, then pull yourself in.

Swamped Boat Drill

To practice swamped boat procedures, you will need to capsize a rowboat. Under the direct supervision of your counselor, begin by bringing in the oars and dropping the locks. Hold the gunwale on one side and put your weight on the far gunwale so that you pull the boat up and over. As the boat comes up on its side and begins to roll over, move out of the boat so that it does not come down on top of you. Do not release your hold on the gunwale at any time during the practice capsize.

If you are having difficulty capsizing the boat simply by leaning, put both hands on one gunwale and stand on the opposite side of the boat. When you rock the boat up with your weight on your feet, you will roll it over. As the boat comes over, move out from under it while maintaining your grip on the gunwale. If you are capsizing with a buddy, be sure to coordinate and communicate.

If you capsize a rowing shell, the same important rule applies—stay with the boat. The recreational shells recommended for use in Scouting have substantial buoyancy. They also are self-righting and self-bailing, and they usually have no loose gear. (On some shells, the seat may separate from the runners.) Before capsizing a rowing shell, position the oars alongside the boat to minimize the risk of boat or oar damage, or personal injury.

Overboard—rolling

Overboard—securing

Overboard—entering

Overboard—swinging into position

Overboard—securing feet

To reboard a capsized shell in deep water, bring the oars close to the boat and roll the boat over. Then secure the oar handles together with the oar blades in the safety position. On some shells, you can remove the foot straps and use them to bind the oar handles together. If you cannot use the foot straps, you can use whatever clothing or other material might be handy. Then use both hands to pull yourself across the cockpit and roll into the center of the boat.

If you have no way to secure the handles together, board by positioning yourself at midship just ahead of the riggers, facing the stern. Hold the oar handles together with one hand. Rather than lifting yourself up and over, slide over the edge of the cockpit, keeping your body low and maintaining your grip on the oar handles. Although the boat may tip sideways as you press down, if the oars stay in the safety position, the boat will right itself as you step in.

If there is another boat on the water that can help you, have the other boaters approach the stern of your shell and hold it firmly upright while you come in over the side. Obviously, those helping you need to be in a rowboat or other stable craft from which they can reach over the side and hold your stern. A skilled rower in a shell may be able to assist by putting the back half of his or her shell alongside and against the back half of your shell and holding your stern tight against his or her midship with one hand while maintaining the oars in e safety position with the other. Even experienced rowers ay occasionally capsize in shells, so you should always have meone in a fixed-seat rowboat or powerboat on the water to sist you.

If you capsize in a canoe rowing rig and the craft swamps, member to stay with the boat—hang on, do not lose contact ith the canoe. Slide over the gunwale to an open area of the craft. Sit flat the bottom and use one oar to pad-e to shore where you can empty the noe and relaunch.

you are overboard in deep water d the canoe rowing rig is still afloat, enter using the flop-over method. egin by placing the oar blades on a eastplate out of your way. Then move ong the gunwale to a midship point here there is an open compartment.

each over the gunwale and place your hands flat on the bottom of canoe at edge of lge. Straighten your arms so the canoe leans toward you.

Duck your head, kick hard, bend one arm and drop your shoulder, and prepare to roll your hips over the gunwale.

Tuck your feet and legs and roll over the gunwale, with your head and shoulder making first contact with the canoe bottom.

Land flat on your back with your spine over the keel, your head extending under the thwart, and your feet and knees high. Lay on the bottom until the canoe steadies and you catch your breath. Then move to your rowing position and get under way.

Boat Rescue

Boat rescues are an important part of lifesaving methods taught and closely followed in all Scouting aquatics. A boat rescue calls for swift action, good boatmanship, and proper caution.

Fixed-seat rescue—a quick launch from shore.

Fixed-seat rescue—step in over the transom.

Fixed-seat rescue—move to midship rowing position watching victim.

Fixed-seat rescue—Out oars watching victim.

Fixed-seat rescue—row toward the victim.

Fixed-seat rescue—pivot at a safe distance from the victim.

Fixed-seat rescue—backwater cautiously to calm the victim.

Fixed-seat rescue—tow the victim to shallow water.

BSA aquatics protection standards require that a rescue boat be on the water for any open-water swimming activity or overboard boating procedure. The same supervision and protection are required during recreational boating activities.

If a fixed-seat rowboat is positioned on the beach for rescue use, it should have oars and PFDs in the boat and should be tied or beached bow out for the quickest response. If the beach has a gradual slope, pull the stern up onto the beach so there is no risk of drifting and where it can quickly be lifted at the transom and pushed out onto the water. Ideally, the stern should be firmly beached with the bow floating on the water and tied (if necessary) with a quick-release hitch.

When a quick launch from shore is necessary, grab the
transom of the beach rowboat, check quickly to be sure that
PFDs and oars are in the boat, lift the transom, and run the
boat out into shallow water until there is sufficient depth to
board over the transom without grounding. Step in with your
hands on the gunwales, keep your weight low and centered,
then quickly turn and sit on the midship seat.

Remember to keep sight of the person who needs help and
to push the bow of the boat in the direction you want to go.
Use this forward momentum to your advantage while you get
in position and prepare to row. As soon as you are seated, slip
on the PFD and put the oars in the out position. Look over your
shoulder to fix your direction toward the person in the water
and begin rowing.

Always make your approach to a swimmer into the
wind or against the current. This allows you to keep
full control of the boat. Remember also that waves
or rough water can make launching from shore
dangerous. Wait for the right moment to launch the
boat. Usually, a comparatively mild interval will
follow a series of heavy waves.

For a fast start, make short, quick strokes to build momentum and then lengthen into your full stroke. Remember to look
over your shoulder after every two or three strokes to be sure
the person in the water is still in sight and you are headed correctly. Keep on course by sighting over the stern. When you are
within one boat length of the person in the water, pivot and
hold water with your transom toward the subject, maintaining
a distance of 8 to 10 feet.

Communicate with the swimmer to determine if he or
she can respond to instructions. Throw your spare PFD to the
person in the water. Remember to consider current and wind
conditions before making your throw. If the person responds
well to instructions, have the swimmer grab the PFD and hold
it close to the chest so that he or she is fully supported and in
no danger.

If you have a buddy helping you with the rescue, you can
make the shore launch even more quickly. Jump into the boat
and move forward, still watching the swimmer, while your passenger runs the boat out and then climbs in over the transom.

Watch the swimmer until the passenger is positioned and shouts, "Ready." Then give way. The passenger, sitting on the transom seat, should keep an eye on the swimmer and use hand signals to direct you to the person. On a signal fro the passenger, pivot the boat. Your passenger should assist the swimmer.

The two-person procedure is preferable because someone is always watching the swimmer, and the oarsman can control the boat while the passenger assists the swimmer. Also, the passenger can hold the swimmer in place while the oarsman rows the boat to shore.

If you are boarding a rescue boat from a pier, push off from the pier as soon as you are in the boat and have moved your rowing position. Once you clear the dock and can begin rowing, do so with short, quick strokes.

If the rescue boat is maintained ready at the dock, it should be secured with a quick-release hitch and positioned so that it is headed, or very easily headed, out.

Before attempting to make contact with the swimmer, sh your oars, put down the locks, and move to the stern of your boat. Kneel on the bottom with your thighs against the transc seat and extend a reach pole or oar to the swimmer. If the pe son responds well to your directions and does not panic, brin him or her to the stern of your boat by pulling in the oar or reach pole, hand over hand. Make contact with the swimmer and lay the person's arms over the transom with his or her hands on the transom seat.

Do not bring the person into the boat. Ask whether he o she can hang on without help. If so, have the swimmer reach up to hold on to the front edge of the transom seat with both hands, with the top edge of the transom under the arms and against the chest. This position lets you see the swimmer's fa and anticipate whether the person is about to pass out or lose his or her grip. If necessary, you can hold the person's hand against the edge of the seat with your foot while rowing.

If the swimmer is merely tired but fully able to maintain his or her grip on the boat while you row, the person can stay down in the water and hold on to the transom. This position creates less drag as you row. Row in until the swimmer can gain footing and no longer needs the boat for support.

If you have a swimmer in tow and are approaching a pier or dock, pivot when you are within a boat length or two of the dock and backwater until you are 4 or 5 feet from the dock. At this point, hold water and instruct the person to turn and reach for the dock. Do not backwater into the dock and bump the swimmer's head. Hold your position on the water until you are sure the swimmer is safely at the dock.

If you are helping an unconscious person or someone who is injured or too weak to hold on to the boat while being towed, you can tie the person in place using a painter or other lashing material (belt, lanyard, or bandanna), or you can bring the person into the boat. If you can quickly secure the person for towing, this is always preferable to bringing someone onboard.

Canoe rig rescue—follow the same approach and tow procedures as in other craft.

In a rowing shell or canoe rowing rig, you can assist a tired swimmer following the same procedure as in a fixed-seat craft—row to the swimmer, pivot, and backwater your stern to where the swimmer can grab the boat while talking and calming the person. Tow the swimmer to shallow water.

Rough-Water Maneuvers

The craft used in BSA rowing activities are not intended for use on rough water. Even a medium chop can rock the boat, making it very difficult to effectively use the oars. You should never set out during a storm or when the water is rough.

 Before an outing, check the weather. If you do not have experience with weather patterns in the area, talk with someone who does. Do not take chances if the weather is uncertain. When you are on the water, stay within a reasonable distance of the shore and keep an eye to the sky for any signs of approaching storms or weather changes.

Even though you should always take every precaution to avoid rough water and storm conditions, weather can change quickly. You should be prepared to deal with unexpected rough conditions so that you can get your craft back to shore as quickly as possible. If you get caught out in a storm, sit as low in the boat as possible, preferably on the bottom. This increases the stability of the boat. If you take on water, bail with whatever you have available. Hold on so that you are stable, with the boat balanced.

If you are making headway, steer the boat into the waves at a slight angle, not head-on. This will reduce pounding. Do not let the boat go sideways into the waves. If you are sideways and wallowing in the troughs of the waves, there is a much greater chance of capsizing. If you are in a rowboat with a transom and your stern is headed into the waves, you are more likely to take on water from waves breaking over the transom.

If it is impossible to make headway, it might help to trail a bucket, a drogue, a sea anchor, or whatever you have that will cause a dragging effect. This will keep the bow headed into the wind, prevent wallowing in the trough, and reduce the drift of your boat downwind.

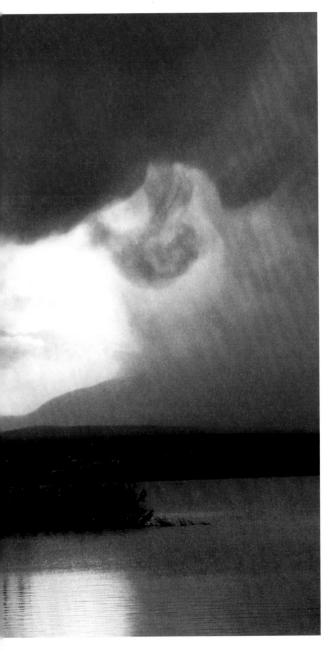

The best and safest rule for rough water is to get ashore. Be aware of approaching storms and head for safety before the weather breaks.

Rowing for Fun and Exercise

Rowing may appear to target only the upper body, but in fact it gives the whole body a thorough workout. In addition to being an excellent form of aerobic exercise, rowing is also a great way to get outside and enjoy the outdoors. You can spend a lazy day out in the middle of a lake fishing, watching wildlife, or just hanging out with your friends. You also can join a rowing team and experience the camaraderie of working toward a goal and the thrill of crossing the finish line with your buddies, knowing that all your hard work has paid off.

Tandem Rowing

If you want to reach your full potential as a rower and team member, find a dedicated partner and practice tandem rowing. Paired-oar rowing in a standard fixed-seat rowboat is a challenge worthy of even the best rower.

Practice for several hours with or without a coxswain, and you will be able to put on a good show. If you have a coxswain on the transom seat, with the oarsmen on the midship and bow seats, the coxswain will call signals and set the course. The coxswain signals so that the oarsman in the bow position can see and understand them. If you are rowing tandem without a coxswain, the bow oarsman calls the signals and the sternman sets the pace.

ndem rowing

rew Rowing

coming part of a rowing team can be an exciting and reward-
g experience. Crew rowing is increasingly popular among
gh school groups in many communities in the United States.
addition, a number of colleges offer scholarships to competi-
e rowers.

If your school does not sponsor a rowing team, look for
ams sponsored by community groups or rowing clubs. Often
rmer college rowers and recreational rowers will form clubs
encourage rowing. They may provide equipment and instruc-
n to new members. These same members, as parents, then
rm junior rowing teams and encourage competition with
her rowing teams in the area.

Race events may have hundreds of different races, but there are only six basic boat configurations. Sweep rowers com in pairs (2s), fours (4s), and eights (8s). Scullers row in single (1x), doubles (2x), and quads (4x). Sweep rowers may or may not carry a coxswain to steer the boat and serve as the on-the-water coach. All eights have coxswains, but pairs, quads, and fours may or may not. The coaches will help you determine which boat configuration will be best suited to your skill and experience level.

Crew rowers are identified by their position in the boat. The rower sitting in the bow is the No. 1 seat or bow seat. The next rower seated with his back to the No. 1 rower is No. 2, then No. 3, and so on. The rower closest to the stern is known as the stroke. The stroke must be a strong rower with excellent technique who sets the rhythm of the boat for the re of the rowers.

Crew rowers speak in terms of strokes per minute (SPM), literally the number of strokes the boat completes in a minute time. The stroke rate at the start is high—38–45, even into the 50s for an eight—and then "settles" to a race cadence typically in the 30s. Crews sprint to the finish, taking the rate up once again. Crews may call for a "Power 10" during the race—a demand for the crew's most intense 10 strokes.

When you're watching a race look for the crew that's mak ing it look easy. They are most likely the ones doing the best job. Look for a continuous, fluid motion from the rowers: synchronization in the boat, clean catches, and the boat with the most consistent speed.

In crew rowing, teamwork is the most important aspect. Rowing isn't a great sport for athletes looking for MVP status. You learn Teamwork with a capital "T." The athlete trying to stand out in an eight will only make the boat slower. The crew made up of individuals willing to work together for a common goal will likely win the race.

Crew rowing—Teamwork is required for the launch.

Crew rowing—
Four-man sweep
crew with cox-
swain in bow.

Crew rowing—
"Stroke" rower
in stern sets
rhythm.

Crew rowing—
"Teamwork"
overtakes the
leader in
competition.

owing for Exercise

'hen you use a sliding-seat boat, rowing is a nearly perfect
ll-body aerobic exercise that gives all the major muscle groups
good workout and develops strength, coordination, and car-
ovascular health. Rowing a standard fixed-seat rowboat is an
cellent upper-body conditioner and is particularly good for
ning and tightening the midsection. It also can help strengthen
e lower back. The stretching and flexing of the muscles of the
wer back can relieve soreness many people develop, often as
e result of inactivity. In addition, rowing is a low-impact sport
at is easier on the cartilage and joints than many other sports,
ch as running, tennis, and downhill skiing.

Rowing Resources

Scouting Literature

Fieldbook; Deck of First Aid; Basic Illustrated Wilderness First Aid; Emergency First Aid pocket guide; Be Prepared First Aid Book; Safety Afloat pamphlet; Sea Scout Manual; Canoeing, Motorboating, and Small-Boat Sailing merit badge pamphlets

Visit the Boy Scouts of America's official retail Web site at *http://www.scoutstuff.org* for a complete listing of all merit badge pamphlets and other helpful Scouting materials and supplies.

Books

Boyne, Daniel J. *Essential Sculling: An Introduction to Basic Strokes, Equipment, Boat Handling, Technique, and Power.* The Lyons Press, 2000.

Churbuck, D. C. *The Book of Rowing.* Overlook Press, 2003.

Cunningham, Frank. *The Sculler at Ease.* Grandview Street Press, 1997.

Halberstam, David. *The Amateurs: The Story of Four Young Men and Their Quest for an Olympic Gold Medal.* Ballantine Books, 1996.

Maybery, Keith. *Rowing: The Essential Guide to Equipment and Techniques.* Stackpole Books, 2002.

McArthur, John. *High Performance Rowing.* Trafalgar Square Publishing, 1997.

Thompson, Luke. *Essential Boating for Teens.* Children's Press, 2000.

Magazines

Rowing News
P.O. Box 831
Hanover, NH 03755
Telephone: 603-643-0059
Web site: *http://www.rowingnews.com*

Organizations and Web Sites

Amateur Rowing Association
Web site: *http://www.ara-rowing.org*

Boathouse Finder
Web site:
http://www.bhfinder.com

USRowing
201 S. Capitol Ave., Suite 400
Indianapolis, IN 46225
Toll-free telephone: 800-314-4769
Web site: *http://www.usrowing.org*

World Rowing
Web site: *http://www.fisa.org*

Acknowledgments

The Boy Scouts of America has promoted rowing and taught rowing skills since its founding, and it continues today with that commitment. This new edition of the *Rowing* merit badge pamphlet was written by K. Gregory Tucker, Readyville, Tennessee, and Daniel G. McGuire, Memphis, Tennessee, who gratefully acknowledge the assistance of Bill Hall, Marietta, Georgia; Walter Person, Memphis, Tennessee; the St. Andrew Rowing Club, Atlanta, Georgia; and Gary Piantedosi, West Acton, Massachusetts. The writers also thank rowing mentor and Scouter James Dalton, Acworth, Georgia, who first helped hone their rowing skills at the BSA National Camping School in 1965.

We appreciate the Quicklist Consulting Committee of the Association for Library Service to Children, a division of the American Library Association, for its assistance with updating the resources section of this merit badge pamphlet.

Photo and Illustration Credits

Dave Bell, courtesy—page 17 *(right)*

©Photos.com—pages 8, 27, and 89

All other photos and illustrations not mentioned above are the property of or are protected by the Boy Scouts of America.

Sam Kolich—cover *(lake)*

John McDearmon—all illustrations on pages 9–10, 20–24, 30, 32–34, 36–39, 46–48, and 57–58

Brian Payne—cover *(PFD);* pages 17 *(left)* and 18 *(top and center right)*

Randy Piland—page 19

The BSA thanks Willie Black, education manager, USRowing, for his assistance with reviewing the manuscript, photos, and illustrations for this new edition of the *Rowing* merit badge pamphlet. We appreciate Mr. Black's input and expertise very much. USRowing serves as the national governing body for the sport of rowing in the United States, as recognized by the U.S. Olympic Committee. USRowing serves more than 14,000 individuals and 900 organizations across the country, helping to ensure that rowing events are conducted safely. Visit the USRowing Web site at *http://www.usrowing.org.*